T0142667

Let's Play DID-YOU-DO!

Starring Karl, Dylan and Fudge

DORET DYKSTRA

Illustrators and actors K Dykstra and D Dykstra

To Mrs England
for our very first English lessons
and
Mister Ridley
for teaching us our first words for reading.

ISBN: Softcover 978-1-5434-0492-0
EBook 978-1-5434-0491-3

Printable information available on the last page.

Rev. date: 04/03/2019

To order additional copies of this book, contact:
Xlibris
1-800-455-039
www.xlibris.com.au
Orders@Xlibris.com.au

Contents

'I recommend the use of 'Let's Play DID-YOU-DO!' as a grammar reference book in any classroom or at home - with more than a hundred high frequency words all in one story and easy to follow activities and grammar games.'

Mrs H Paulus, B Prim Ed

'Let's Play DID-YOU-DO!' is a delightfully different way to introduce children to the complexities of English grammar. It is always fun for children to learn with other children and the children in the illustration soon become friends with the reader. It is easy to empathise with them. Although best suited to second language learners, it will also be accessible and useful to first language English speakers who will enjoy the story and characters so much, they will hardly know that they are learning.

Michael Bräsler B SC, H.Dip (ed), B A (Hons)

Let's Play DID-YOU-DO!

Learn to speak English and practise your grammar skills too!

by Doret Dykstra

Illustrators and actors

Karl Dykstra and Dylan Dykstra

If you are learning English as your second language, the story 'Let's Play DID-YOU-DO!' is for you!

This story was written to convey the meanings of more than a hundred words we say often. The words we say often are also the words we need for reading.

If you are still learning to read, someone should work with you.

Once you understand all the words you need for speaking and reading you can start playing the games with the boys and their dog, Fudge.

You will practise your listening skills and find the answers to all your questions and improve your grammar skills for writing.

I need all these words for reading but what do they mean?

The words we say often are called 'High Frequency Words', but we don't hear them that often if we don't speak English at home.

If you are still learning to speak English, ask someone to read this story for you. Discuss what happens in the story with someone who speaks your language. Then read it again and look at the pictures. Say the words. Then look at the list below. Start with the words in the first column and look at the pages in the story where the word is used. You will be able to discover their meaning by looking at the pictures.

Page number from story	Word or sentence from that page in the story
26,29	her
5	I
2,6	it
2,5,6	my
25,26	she
2	we
9,34	they

Page number from story	Word or sentence from that page in the story
6	our
34	their
32	us
31	you
6	your

Page number from story	Word or sentence from that page in the story
2,24	a
24	an
7,10	any
5,9	some
2,20	that
15,21	the
4	these
2	this
4,15,33	those

Page number from story	Word or sentence from that page in the story
7,20	now
6,11	then

Page number from story	Word or sentence from that page in the story
7,20	am
4,9	are
2,26,31	is
6,7,31	can
10,11,14,31	do
2,5,26	have

Page number from story	Word or sentence from that page in the story
13	was
21	were
24	did
18,23	could
27	should
5,27	will

Page number from story	Word or sentence from that page in the story
28,33	again
4	also
15,24	too

Page number from story	Word or sentence from that page in the story
7,32,33	of
18,23	as
15	at
2	so

Page number from story	Word or sentence from that page in the story
23,28,33	no
2,15	not
6	yes

Page number from story	Word or sentence from that page in the story
26	answer
28,30	come
27	get
11,13	go
31	know
20	like
15	look
2,5	said
23	set
17	shout
23	show
6	tell
25,27	think
24	wait
17,31	want
25,34	went

Page number from story	Word or sentence from that page in the story
23,29	back
27	down
15	end
2	first
17	up

Page number from story	Word or sentence from that page in the story
28,29	here
26	near
13,21,26	there

Page number from story	Word or sentence from that page in the story
23	into
29	on
26	over
12	to
2	under
2,15,30	with

Page number from story	Word or sentence from that page in the story
2,6	and
32	but
4	for

Page number from story	Word or sentence from that page in the story
6,11	how
6	what
25	where
2	which
9	who
24	why

Page number from story	Word or sentence from that page in the story
2	easy
29	good
2	little
14	mad
13	together
9	very

Page number from story	Word or sentence from that page in the story
23	thing

Once you understand the meaning of all these words move to the activities at the end of this story and practise your grammar skills.

It is not so easy to have a picnic with my brother and our little dog, Fudge. First, we have to agree on which tree to sit under.
'This tree.' I said.
'Or that tree.' my brother said.

Finally... we agreed.

We also don't eat the same things.
That is my brother's banana.
These are
my grapes.
Those biscuits
are for Fudge.

'I don't actually
like bananas,'
my brother said.
'I will have some biscuits
with little Fudge instead.'
Smiggle
Smiggle

'Let's play something.' I said.

'What?' my brother asked.

'Let's play "ANYTHING".' I said.

'Anything?' my brother asked.

'Yes, "ANYTHING" is the name of our game.'

'That rhymes you know.' my brother said.
'How do you play it?'

'I close my eyes and tell you what I see.
It can be anything. You then tell me what
I saw and then it is your turn.'

'I see lots of aliens.'
'Can you see any people?' my brother asked.
'No, I am in space.' I said.
'Ok, you saw aliens. Now it is my turn.'

'I see a monster.'
'You saw a monster. My turn.'

'I see three people who are very ill.'
'That's funny. You saw three people who were very ill... They probably ate some of your grapes!'
smiggle
smiggle

'You don't like eating any fruit, do you?'
'No, I don't. My turn.'
smiggle
smiggle

'Let's play something else.'
'Something else?' my brother asked.
'Yes, let's play "ANYWHERE".' I said.
'How do you play "ANYWHERE"?'
'I close my eyes and go somewhere… anywhere.
You then tell me where I went and then it is your turn.'

'I go to school to learn how to read.' I said.

'Oh, no! You went to school! My turn.' my brother said.

'That's unfair.' I said.

'Why?' my brother asked.

'It was unfair because I was still there and then you said "My turn!" again.' I explained.
'Ok. It is still your turn then.'
'Let's go there together.' I said.

'Are you mad? I don't want to go to school!'

‘Did you know the
word “look”
looks like 100
with a “k” at the end?’
100k
‘Can you read all those words?’
my brother asked.
‘Not yet.’ I said.
‘Me too.’

'I see two clouds. It is raining...'

'Look! It is raining numbers...'

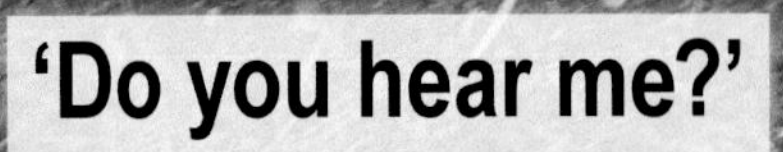

'Hey, what are you up to?' I shouted. 'You tricked me! I thought we were still playing "ANYWHERE".'
'I want to play rugby instead.' my brother said.

'Ok then, tackle me!' I shouted and started running with the ball as fast as I could.

I am kicking
the ball.

We are running
and passing the
ball to each other.

He is throwing
the ball.

'I am tired now.'
'Let's play
"DID-YOU-DO".
I like playing that game.'
my brother said.

'Ok, your turn. What did you do yesterday?'
'I swam in the sea. There were gigantic waves.'

'Your turn. What did you do yesterday?' I asked.
"I drew four turtles and painted a fish.'
my brother said.
'Wow!'

'What? There is no such thing as a hammerhead jellyfish.' my brother said.

'Yes, there is.' I said.

'No, there isn't.' my brother said.

'Yes, there is. I couldn't show you because I set it free. I threw it back into the ocean.'

'Wait a minute. Did you close your eyes too?' my brother asked.
'Yes, why?'
'I didn't ask you what you did. You were supposed to keep an eye on Fudge.'
'Oops!' I said.

I think she went that way.’

‘I think she went this way.’

'There she is!' my brother shouted.

'Where?' I asked.

'Over there! Near the river...' my brother answered.

'Let's run, we have to catch her!'

'I think we should roll down the hill, we will get there faster!'

'Fudge! Come here!'

'Oh no, she is running
that way again!' I shouted.

'Careful. That's it. Good dog.
Here is your treat, little Fudge.'
my brother said.
'I've got her.
Quick, put her
leash back on.'

'Come little Fudge. We will play a game with you.'

'Do you want to play cards, Fudge?'
my brother asked.

'Don't be silly. She can't
read. She is a dog.' I said.
'I know what we can do.
Let's play
"ROUNDABOUT"
with Fudge.'
I like playing that game.
STEEDEN
NRL

We are walking around the tree.

Sometimes all of us are in front of the tree.

Sometimes one of us is behind the tree.

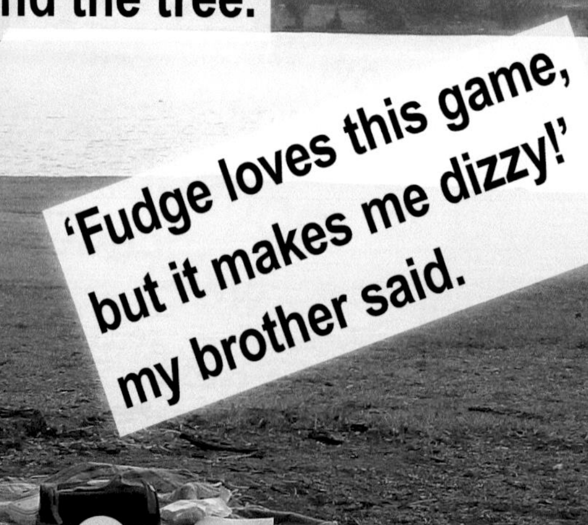

'Fudge loves this game, but it makes me dizzy!' my brother said.

'Let's play somewhere else.'
I said.
'Oh no, not again!' my brother said.
'Not another one of those games.'

No silly, I meant
et's go somewhere
lse.' I said.
'Ah, I see. Let's go
somewhere else
and play there.'

They took their bags and off they went.
'No, we are not looking for another tree!'
'This way, Fudge!'

Grammar guide index:

GRAMMAR GAMES:

Some 'High Frequency Words' are very confusing! The more you read 'Let's Play DID-YOU-DO!' the easier the meaning of these words will be.

- Play the game **ROUNDABOUT** on page 32 by walking around an object like a tree or a chair and discover the meaning of these words that show position:

32	around
32	behind
32	in front of

- Look at the pictures on these pages and discover the difference between the words below:

2	this	One thing close to you.	4	these	More than one thing close to you.
2,4	that	One thing further away.	4,15	those	More than one thing further away.

- When do I use **'to'** and when do I use **'too'**?

We use **'to'** with the words **'have'**, **'go'**, **'want'** and **'supposed'**:

We have **to** agree.	2
I go **to** school.	12
I want **to** play rugby.	17
You were supposed **to** keep an eye on Fudge.	24
We have **to** catch her.	26

The word **'too'** has the same meaning as the word 'also', but is used at the end of the sentence.

Me **too**.	15	Did you close your eyes **too**?	24

So, if you would also like to play the game you would say: I want to play, too.

Remember the spelling of the number 2.

I see **two** clouds.	16

- When do I use **'for'** and when do I use **'four'**?

Those biscuits are **for** Fudge.	4	
We are not looking **for** another tree.	34	
I drew **four** turtles.	22	The spelling of the number 4.

- Do I have to change 'he' to **'him'**? Yes, in the same way you would change 'she' to **'her'**, 'we' to **'our'**, 'I' to **'my'**, 'you' to **'your'** and 'they' to **'their'**.

There **he** is. We have to catch **him.**

There **she** is. (Fudge is female)

26	We have to catch **her**.

We are playing a game called: 'ANYTHING'.	6	'ANYTHING' is the name of **our** game.
I have a turn and then **you** have a turn.	6	It is **my** turn first and then it is **your** turn.
They have bags that they have to take home with them.	34	They took **their** bags and off they went.

➢ When do I use **'a'** and when do I use **'an'**? It depends on the pronunciation of the next word. The words 'monster' and 'jellyfish' are pronounced with a consonant sound, but 'eye' and 'alien' are pronounced with a vowel sound.

a	monster	8
a	jellyfish	23

but

an	eye	24
an	alien	

On page 7 the boy saw lots of aliens, but if he saw only one alien his words would have been: 'I saw **an** alien.'

Another example: **'an** M & M sweetie' – the letter M is pronounced with a vowel sound.

➢ When do I use **'of'** and when do I use **'off'**?

lots **of** aliens	7

OR a lot **of** aliens

another one **of**	33

in front **of**	32
one **of** us	32
all **of** us	32

They took their bags and **off** they went.	34

The word **'off'** has a different meaning as in the sentence above. They have to take their bags away with them. (Another example: Switch the light **off**.)

I take my hat off for you! You are doing a great job and working on improving your English. Well done! You are almost ready to start working on some difficult grammar skills.

➢ Read the story again to discover the meaning of these more difficult words commonly used in everyday English. See if you can discover their meaning by looking at the context of these words in the story.

5	actually
3	finally
15	not yet
9	probably
32	sometimes

13	because
5,17	instead

33,34	another
19	each other
13	together

6	anything
11	anywhere
6,11	something/ something else
11,33	somewhere / somewhere else

Now that you are familiar with more than a hundred words we often use in English and their meaning, we can look at the following questions and practise our basic grammar skills.

Why is there a comma in the air?

- Sometimes it shows that something belongs to someone.

4	my **brother's** banana	The banana belongs to my brother.

- Sometimes it is the short version for two words that are put together.

6, 13	let's

let us	**Let's** play something. **Let's** play "ANYTHING". **Let's** go there together.

- Helping verbs like 'is' and 'have' are also shortened in this way when we speak and in writing we replace some of the letters in the word with an apostrophe or a comma in the air.

9,12,29	that's
29	I've

that is	**That's** funny. **That's** unfair. **That's** it.
I have	**I've** got her.

- In English the word **'not'** is put together with the helping verbs and then shortened by putting a comma where the 'n' and the 'o' is left out.

23	isn't
10	don't
24	didn't
23	couldn't
31	can't

is not	No, there **isn't**.
do not	You **don't** like eating any fruit. No I **don't**.
did not	I **didn't** ask you what you did.
could not	I **couldn't** show you.
can not	She **can't** read.

- Sometimes it is used for punctuation.

""	6	inverted commas	'Yes, "ANYTHING" is the name of our game.'
''	24	speech marks	'Oops!' I said.
		Other punctuation marks:	
-	Title	colon	Let's Play DID-YOU-DO!
,	23	comma	Yes, there is.
!	25	exclamation mark	Oh no!
?	25	question mark	Where is Fudge?

Does spelling really matter?

Yes, sometimes words may even sound the same but are spelt differently. Read these pages and look at the difference in meaning between:

6,15,31	know
33	no

33	see
21	sea

4,34	for
22	four

13,21,26,27,33	there
34	their

12,14	to
15,24	too
16	two

16	hear
28,29	here

Look at the spelling of all these words used in the story:

29	care**ful**

1	lit**tle**
18	tack**le**
22	turt**les**

27	fast**er**

24	min**ut**e

28	ag**ain**
12	unf**air**

5	actu**ally**
3	fin**ally**
33	si**lly**

19	ba**ll**
27	hi**ll**
27	ro**ll**
14,17	sti**ll**
6	te**ll**
27	wi**ll**

2	**F**udge

17	thou**ght**

23	fr**ee**
9	thr**ee**
2	tr**ee**

26	cat**ch**
19	ea**ch**
23	su**ch**
2	whi**ch**

12	s**ch**ool

29	tr**ea**t
23	oc**ea**n
29	l**ea**sh

29	q**ui**ck

24	su**pp**osed
28	ru**nn**ing

23	ba**ck**
2	pi**c**ni**c**
21	gigant**ic**

Can I say I 'is'? No, we say I <u>am</u>.

20	I **am** tired.	31	She **is** a dog.
32	One of us **is** behind the tree.	32	All of us **are** in front of the tree

Let's start with the basics. In English we use the helping verbs **AM**, **IS**, **ARE**, **DO**, **HAS** and **HAVE** to help us say when things happen. When we talk about the past these verbs change to **WAS**, **WERE**, **DID** and **HAD**.

- AM IS ARE   These words change in the PAST to: WAS WERE

PRESENT

I	am
He, She, The dog	is
We, You, They	are

PAST

I	was
He, She, The dog	was
We, You, They	were

It is important to remember when things happen. Let's look at page 20 and read the sentences in the first column. Then close the book and change them to the past.

What happened on page 20?

Present	Past
I **am** tired	I **was** tired.
He **is** tired. The dog **is** tired.	He **was** tired. She **was** tired.
We **are** tired.	We **were** tired after playing all those games.

Do the same with these sentences: What happened on these pages?

Page	Present	Past
4	This **is** my brother's banana.	That **was** my brother's banana.
4	Those biscuits **are** for Fudge.	Those biscuits **were** for Fudge.
6	It **is** your turn.	It **was** your turn.

- DO/DOES

PRESENT

He, She, It, The dog	does		My brother doesn't like eating bananas, **does** he? No, he doesn't. He said:
I	do	5	'I don't actually like eating bananas.'
You	do		I **do**. **Do** you?

What about Fudge? She **doesn't** like fruit.

- DO and DOES change in the PAST to DID.

PAST

He, She, It, The dog	did
You, We, They	did

Look at these sentences: Change the sentences to the past.

Page	Present	Past
16	**Do** you hear me? **Does** he hear me?	**Did** you hear me? **Did** he hear me?
6	How **do** you play it?	How **did** you play it?

- HAVE HAS Both of these words change in the PAST to HAD.

PRESENT

I	have
He, She, It The dog	has

PAST

I	had
He, She, It The dog	had

You, We, They	have

You, We, They	had

Look at page 2 and 4. Read the first column. Then close the book and say what happened on these pages.

2	First, we **have** to agree. I **have** to agree. He **has** to agree. The dog **has** to agree.	We all **had** to agree on which tree to sit under.
2,4	We **have** a picnic. I **have** some grapes. My brother **has** a banana. Fudge **has** biscuits.	We **had** a picnic. I **had** some grapes. They **had** some biscuits.

What about the future?

Well, in the future we use the word 'will'.

I	will
He, She, It,The dog	will
You, We, They	will

5	I **will** have some biscuits with Fudge instead.	They **will** have some biscuits.
27	We **will** get there faster.	I **will** get there faster and he **will** get there faster.
30	We **will** play a game with you.	**I will** play a game with you. **She will** play a game with you. **He will** play a game with you.

Why do verbs change in so many ways?

It is just the way it is. You have to remember when it happens and then follow the grammar rules.

- In the present we add an 's' when we talk about one person or thing.

15	The word 'look'	look**s**	like '100' with a 'k' at the end.	One word
32	Fudge	love**s**	this game.	One dog
32	It	make**s**	me dizzy.	One game

Remember, although 'I' am one person we still say **'I think'** and **'I see'** and **not** 'I ~~thinks~~' or 'I ~~sees~~'!

27	I think	He think**s**	She think**s**	The dog think**s**	**but**	We They You	think
33	I see	He see**s**	She see**s**	The dog see**s**	**but**	We They You	see

- When do I add **'-ing'** at the end of a verb?

Well, when something is busy happening. Look at these pages to see what is happening. This is called the present continuous.

16	It **is** rain**ing**.	28	She **is** runn**ing**.	32	We **are** walk**ing**.

34	We **are** not look**ing** for another tree!

Look at page 19. They **are playing** rugby (also known as 'footy').

19	I **am** kick**ing** the ball.	We **are** runn**ing** and pass**ing** the ball.	He **is** throw**ing** the ball.

- We also add **'-ing'** when something was happening in the past. This is called the past continuous.

17	I thought we **were** still play**ing** 'ANYWHERE?'
23	I went fish**ing**.

Remember the word '**go**' changes to '**went**' in the past. You will learn more about this later in the section about irregular verb changes.

Close the book and say what happened on page 19. They **were playing** rugby.

Practise the past continuous by changing the sentences on these pages to the past.

16	It **was** rain**ing**.	28	She **was** runn**ing**.	32	We **were** walk**ing**.

34	We **were** not look**ing** for another tree!

19	I **was** kick**ing** the ball.	We **were** runn**ing** and pass**ing** the ball.	He **was** throw**ing** the ball.

➢ We also add **'-ing'** after the words 'like' and 'started':

10	You don't **like**	eat**ing**	any fruit, do you?
20	I **like**	play**ing**	that game.
18	I **started**	runn**ing**	as fast as I could.

➢ Do verbs always change in the past? Yes, but not always in the same way.

➢ Sometimes you simply add **'-d'**. Read the sentences on these pages and look at these words:

The verb 'agree' will change to 'agreed'.

3	Finally...we agree**d.**

➢ Sometimes you simply add **'-ed'**. Read the story and look at these words.

	paint		ask		explain		answer
22	paint**ed**	6	ask**ed**	13	explain**ed**	26	answer**ed**

	trick		shout		start
17	trick**ed**	17	shout**ed**	18	start**ed**

Let's play the game **'DID-YOU-DO'** as on pages 20-24 and practise verbs that change in this way.

Close your eyes and think of the verb 'paint'.

Your friend will ask you the following question: *What did you do yesterday?*

Answer by changing the verb to the past: I paint**ed** a fish.

Do the same with the verbs in the columns above and below. Make your own sentences to practise the verb changes by playing this game with a friend.

play	walk	wait	want
play**ed**	walk**ed**	wait**ed**	want**ed**

- Some verbs change completely in the past and are called **irregular verbs.**

Let's play the game **'ANYTHING'** as on page 6-10 with the boys and their dog, Fudge to practise other verbs that change completely.

Close your eyes and say what you 'see'. Your friend then tells you what you 'saw'.

7	I **see** lots of aliens.	You **saw** lots of aliens.

Let's play the game **'ANYWHERE'** as on page 11-14 and practise the change of the word **'go'** to **'went'** in the past.

Close your eyes and think of a place where you usually go. It can be anywhere. Use the sentence 'I go to...' and then your friend will tell you where you 'went'.

12	I **go** to school.	You **went** to school.

A lot of verbs in English change completely in the past. Read the sentences on the following pages and practise these words.

The word 'say' changes to said in the past. Remember the spelling of the word **said**: The 'y' changes to 'i'.

say	2	'This tree.' I **said**. 'Or that tree.' my brother **said**.
think	17	I **thought** we were still playing 'ANYWHERE'.
mean	33	No, silly, I **meant** let's go somewhere else.

The verb 'tell' will change to told. Let's read page 6-7 and then say what happened on that page.

You tell me what I see.	6	You **told** me what I saw.

See how these verbs changed in the story:

eat	9	They **ate** your grapes.
throw	23	I **threw** it back into the ocean.

Now let's practise some of the more difficult irregular verb changes by playing the game **'DID-YOU-DO'** again and using the following verbs.

- Close your eyes and think of the verb 'draw'. Your friend will then ask you:

What did you do yesterday?

draw	22	I **drew** four turtles.

Now practise more irregular changes by using these verbs and make your own sentences. What did you do yesterday?

swim	21	I **swam** in the sea.
catch	23	I **caught** a giant hammerhead jellyfish.
take	34	They **took** their bags and off they went.

Practise the changes of the verbs in the column below by playing the game again and make your own sentences.

Answer by changing the verb to the past e.g.

I **took** a photo.   I **threw** a ball.

All these verbs can even change once more!

Add a third person to the game **'ANYTHING'** to practise the 3rd column of these verbs, by asking a question in surprise. Use the verb in the first column and make a sentence. It can be anything. Your friend changes your sentence into the past and then the third person changes the sentence into the past perfect, using **has** or **have** plus the **3rd column** of the verb.

eat	ate	eaten
draw	drew	drawn
go	went	gone
see	saw	seen
swim	swam	swum
take	took	taken
throw	threw	thrown

Example: I eat a spider.

You ate a spider.

What? Have you just eaten a spider?

It is just a game, we use the word 'just' to emphasise what happened a short while ago and this is called the present perfect tense.

eat	They **ate** your grapes.	eaten	What? Have they just **eaten** your grapes?
draw	He **drew** four turtles.	drawn	What? Has he just **drawn** four turtles?
go	He **went** to school.	gone	What? Has he just **gone** to school?
see	He **saw** a monster.	seen	What? Has he just **seen** a monster?
swim	You **swam** in the sea.	swum	What? Have you just **swum** in the sea?
take	They **took** their bags.	taken	What? Have they just **taken** their bags?
throw	He **threw** the fish back into the sea.	thrown	What? Has he just **thrown** the fish back into the sea?

Remember some verbs change only once, so if we use them in this way the 2nd column of the verb will be the same as the 3rd.

paint	painted	painted
catch	caught	caught

paint	You **painted** a fish.	painted	What? Has he just **painted** a fish?
catch	You **caught** a hammerhead jellyfish.	caught	What? Have you just **caught** a hammerhead jellyfish?

What? Have you worked through all these activity pages?

Congratulations! You now know more than a hundred words you need for speaking, reading and writing in English and you have mastered the basic grammar skills. Well done!

Please note: The very first list of High Frequency Words was compiled by Edward William Dolch in 1936. Many lists exist today. The word list on page 1 was compiled by the author and contains only the High Frequency Words used in the story 'Let's Play DID-YOU-DO!' as well as other everyday words. The grammar pages contain explanations of basic grammar used for the purpose of learning your first grammar skills when learning English as your second language. There are many other grammar rules in English and exceptions to rules which are not covered by this story.

Use the following list of some other everyday verbs and practise all three columns by playing the games.

1st column	2nd column	3rd column
bite	bit	bitten
blow	blew	blown
break	broke	broken
bring	brought	brought
buy	bought	bought
choose	chose	chosen
cut	cut	cut
dig	dug	dug
drink	drank	drunk
drive	drove	driven
fall	fell	fallen
feed	fed	fed
feel	felt	felt
fight	fought	fought
find	found	found
fly	flew	flown
give	gave	given
grow	grew	grown
hear	heard	heard
hide	hid	hidden
hit	hit	hit
keep	kept	kept
know	knew	known
leave	left	left
lose	lost	lost
make	made	made
meet	met	met
pay	paid	paid
put	put	put
ride	rode	ridden
ring	rang	rung
run	ran	run
sell	sold	sold

send	sent	sent
shake	shook	shaken
show	showed	shown
sing	sang	sung
sit	sat	sat
sleep	slept	slept
speak	spoke	spoken
stand	stood	stood
stick	stuck	stuck
tear	tore	torn
win	won	won
write	wrote	written

There are many more verbs in English that can be practised in this way. Eventually you have to know them all so that you are able to use them in all the tenses.

Some verbs like **'hit'**, **'cut'** and **'put'** stays the same for all three columns. Remember the verb **'run'** changes to **'ran'** in the second column and then changes back to the original form **'run'** in the 3rd column.

Through reading 'Let's Play DID-YOU-DO!' you have learnt about the **simple present**, **simple past** and **simple future** tenses, as well as **present continuous, past continuous** and the **present perfect.**

In this story **Fudge runs away**. This is called the **simple present tense.** Let's look at the story again to discover what the **six other tenses** in the English Language sounds like.

By the time the boys open their eyes on page 25, **Fudge will have run away**.

On page 26 **Fudge will be running** even further away.

On page 27 the boys roll down the hill to get to Fudge faster. By the time they get to the river **Fudge will have been running** up and down.

Before Fudge finally stops near the river on page 29, the boys **have been running** up and down after Fudge.

On page 29 they finally put her leash back on. Fudge was tired because she **had been running** up and down.

One page 30 the boys were probably tired too because **they had run** all the way to the river.

Future Continuous	**will be running**	will + be + 1st column of verb + -'ing'
Future Perfect	**will have run**	will + have + 3rd column of verb

Future Perfect Continuous	**will have been running**	will + have + been + 1st column of verb + '-ing'
Present Perfect Continuous	**have been running**	have + been + 1st column of verb + '-ing'
Past Perfect Continuous	**had been running**	had + been + 1st column of verb + '-ing'
Past Perfect	**had run**	had + 3rd column of verb

Let's do an exercise with the verb '**eat**' and change the sentence '**I eat some grapes**.' into all twelve tenses, so that you will always have a diagram to refer back to. It is always important to remember when things happen.

Simple Present	**eat**	I eat lots of grapes. I usually eat some grapes every morning at 9 am.
Present Continuous	**am/is/are eating**	It is 9 am. I am eating some grapes.
Present Perfect Continuous	**have been eating**	9.10 am The phone rings. 'What have you been up to?' asks my friend. 'I have been eating some grapes.' I said.
Present Perfect	**has/have eaten**	9.20 I have eaten some grapes about 5 minutes ago.

Simple Past	**ate**	Yesterday, I ate some grapes too.
Past Continuous	**was/were eating**	Yesterday, at exactly 9, I was eating some grapes.
Past Perfect Continuous	**had been eating**	Yesterday by 9.15 I had been eating grapes for about fifteen minutes.
Past Perfect	**had eaten**	Yesterday, at 9.20 I had already eaten some grapes.

Simple Future	**will eat**	Tomorrow morning I will eat some grapes too.
Future Continuous Tense	**will be eating**	Tomorrow morning at exactly 9 am I will be eating some grapes, again.
Future Perfect Continuous	**will have been eating**	By 9.15 tomorrow morning I will have been eating my daily grapes for about fifteen minutes.
Future Perfect Tense	**will have eaten**	Tomorrow morning at 9.20 I will have eaten some grapes.

See how important it is to get to know all the verb changes so that you will be able to use them in all the twelve tenses in the English Language.

Doret Dykstra, a creative soul with a niche for writing. She has taught English as a Second Language to children and adults from many different nationalities. Having lived in four different countries she fully understands the immigration process and is passionate about helping people cross their second bridge namely communicating in English. With a background in theatre she completed a Diploma in Writing and Publishing for Children and indulges herself in writing stories inspired by the adventures of her twin boys in Australia.

BA DRAMA (UNIV PTA RSA)
CELTA CERTIFICATE IN ENGLISH LANGUAGE TEACHING (Cambridge UK)
DIPLOMA in WRITING and PUBLISHING FOR
CHILDREN (Australian College, NSW)